OUR PITS
OUR POWER
COAL POWER!
Don't let Britain's economy
fade away
SUPPORT THE MINERS - WRITE TO JOHN MAJOR
PRODUCED BY MANSFIELD DISTRICT COUNCIL FOR THE COMMUNITIES OF BRITAIN

COAL
MINING

■ Though five miles from the county border, Bolsover Colliery was officially classed as a Nottinghamshire pit. The reason dated back to the General Strike of 1926. Following the collapse of the strike, Nottinghamshire MP George Spencer, set up the Nottingham & District Miners' Industrial Union; better known as the Spencer Union. The coal owners loved it; a union which promised not to call its members out on strike, to stay out of politics, and to work with the bosses. Many miners hated it. The owners simply declared that from hence forth their mines were Nottinghamshire pits.

INTRODUCTION & ACKNOWLEDGEMENTS

This book, When Coal was King, came about when someone at the Derbyshire Times said: "Why don't we publish some of the stuff on coal mining material that readers have been sending in to us for Mining the Past and flesh it out with pictures and information from our own archives?"

Well, the project got the go ahead and this, for better of worse, is the result.

The book is divided into several sections: Down Pit, On the Surface, On the Move, Accidents & Disasters, Industrial Unrest, and End of an Era? And, before anyone contacts us to us that we have missed things out, this is not a full-blown history book on the mines of north Derbyshire it is a trip down memory lane. In fact it is not even confined the north Derbyshire; several north Nottinghamshire and a couple of nearby South Yorkshire pits have managed to sneak in.

The section headings are self explanatory – well nearly. Down Pit is what it says it is, with pictures and memories from A Winning, Creswell, Bolsover, Markham, and Bevercotes collieries, and a ghost story from Ireland Colliery. We also decide to include a number of images from the well-known Clay Cross postcard series and they appear from time to time allowing our readers to compare what the industry was like in the 1900s with what it was like before it was deliberately destroyed.

On the Surface covers all manner of topics from changing winding wheels at Ireland Colliery to felling trees during the Second World War to make pit props. In one way or another, this section visits at least 17 collieries including: Alfreton, Arkwright, Bevercotes, Bolsover, Brookhouse, Creswell, Dinnington Main, Glapwell, Grassmoor, Harworth, Ireland, Langwith, Shirebrook, Markham, Warsop, Welbeck, and Williamthorpe.

On the Move might be a bit of a surprise to many but in the 1970s it was calculated by the NCB that more than 70 per cent of time at a pit was spent moving things about; coal, spoil, equipment, men and machinery. So it's in this the section where you will find pictures of pit ponies, manriders, shunt engines, winding gear etc.

Accidents & Disasters looks mainly at Creswell in 1950 and Markham in 1973, though we also have a first hand account of rescue work following the Markham explosion in 1938. Industrial Unrest covers the 1972, 1974, and 1984-85 strikes and aftermath.

In the Derbyshire Times for 25 March 2004, it was stated that at the start of the 1984-85 strike there had been 14,500 miners, 11 pits and two area workshops in Derbyshire. The pits and workshops have gone and the once powerful Derbyshire NUM was reduced to renting two rooms in the Saltergate, Chesterfield, building it used to own as its county headquarters. Which brings us nicely to our final selection of pictures in End of an Era?

Many believe that the deliberate run down of UK coal mining; sealing off reserves of nearly 30 billion tonnes, and the privatisation of what remained, was little short of treason. It could be argued that with much of this coal now unreachable, part of the country's energy supply is open to outside interference. There cannot be any logic in importing coal from Australia or wherever to burn in UK power stations when quality coal lies in our own ground. And not all the imported coal was as good as the politicians at first made out; some of it would hardly burn and had to be mixed with British coal at the power stations before it could go on to the furnace conveyors.

There is also another argument in that had mining not been privatised then the NCB's own research establishment might already have delivered viable clean-coal technology. Like British Rail, NCB research was world class; privatisation destroyed both organisations.

In March 2004, Alan Gascoyne, president of the Derbyshire NUM, said: "Because the pits were closed, it doesn't mean to say miners and miners' problems go away."

The area office's small staff helps ex-miners and their dependants with everything from advice on benefits and pensions, to claims for industrial disease, and represent them at tribunals. The union was still trying to look after the interests of people and communities connected with the mining industry.

It is impossible to say what ex-miners do now. Many finished up working in hospitals, factories, and catering. Some have never been able to settle into another job outside the pits. In February 2008, Derbyshire Times reader John Robinson wrote: 'The pit I worked at shut down twenty years ago and I work now in a supermarket, but I am not a shop assistant, I am an ex miner, an ex miner who is extremely proud to have worked in the industry, proud of what I did to earn my daily bread.

'Mining, during the time that I spent in the industry, provided a good standard of living. It supported not only miners but shopkeepers, pubs and many many factories that supplied the industry and kept the wheels turning. Markham Works, alas now is also just another memory and although a union basher and capitalist I bet that Charlie Markham would be spinning in his grave at what has happened to the mining and related industries.

This book would not have been possible without contributions from Derbyshire Times readers, including: Malcolm Cowley, Mrs Cynthia Robinson, Ian Gardner, Derrick Frearson, Stuart Thornley, D. Robotham, Glyn Power, Stephen Brunt, Philip Utridge, Melvyn Whittaker, Alan Wright, Eric Bird, Richard J Adams, Brian Collins, Olwyn Moore, Mrs N Palmer, Mr Clark, John Barry Keyworth, Pete Shaw, Roy Roberts, Mr J P Marsden, John Hill, Joan Isaacs, Beryle Howdle, David J Higgins, Michael Cherry, George Holmes, Clive Pearce, E Walton, J Ward, Councillor G P Ramshaw, Joyce Whittaker, Barbara Hobday, D Buxton, Andrew Jones, Ian Whitworth, Miss Rachael Johnson, Geoffrey Brown, Lynne Davies, S Slibbard, Mr A Price, C Robinson, Mr W Skevington, Stuart J Holmes, and I apologise in advance if I have forgotten anyone; don't take it personally.

Special thanks also go to Chesterfield Local Studies Library, and the library staff, journalists and photographers of the Morning Telegraph, Sheffield Star, Derbyshire Times and Coal News including: Ian Gardner, Michael Lynch, John Winter, Lesley Fields, Guy Harrington, Helen Beighton, David Vaughan and of course Mike Wilson.

Above all, put out the cat, put on the kettle, sit back and enjoy When Coal Was King.

Clive Hardy
2010

DOWN PIT

■ This image was originally published in the well known Clay Cross Company's series of postcards. The men are working a narrow seam; one man getting the coal, the other loading the tub which has the number 12x chalked on its end. This number identified the men, an important piece of information as they were paid by the tub load.

■ Again, this image is taken from the Clay Cross Company postcards (No.103) and shows men engaged in shearing up the roadway. Interestingly, the man in the centre of this picture and the one to the right appear to be the same men as in the previous image. The tub marked 12x is also present.

■ No.123 in the Clay Cross postcard series, this image shows pit deputies carrying out safety checks on the roof and rope haulage. This series of pictures was taken before the outbreak of the Great War; a time when there were more than 160 pits working in Derbyshire alone and giving direct employment to 40,000 men.

■ This is the pit bottom at Ireland Colliery and every word of the following account is true, written down as my memory best recalls it.

When I was a deputy at Ireland during the 1980s it became the practice that some official had to stay in the pit between the afternoon shift going off and the night coming on. This was OK during the week as some of the afternoon shift used to work overtime and there was a late deputy on to cover this. Not so on a Friday as it was customary that two strips of coal had been cut on the faces a concession was granted and the men would be allowed to go home early.

The usual end to the afternoon shift was 8.15pm but the Friday concession meant the men could be out of the mine at any time after about 6.30pm and the first man down the pit on the night shift would be a deputy at about 10.15pm. Consequently on a Friday there was a gap of three or fours hours between the two shifts.

The deputy manager Mr Galloway decided that there should be an official in the pit during the gap so deputies were rostered for this duty.

My time came round to do the cover. All the deputies used to do during this lull between the shifts was read or sleep in their pit bottom cabin which was adjacent to where the old stables had been for the pit ponies, the last of which had been retired back in 1970. On the day I was covering something happened that scared me witless – a really eerie experience. I was in the pit bottom cabin completely on my own in the mine, hundreds of yards away from any other human being. There was no question of anyone else being down there as I had phoned the time office and they had confirmed that the pit was empty.

I was sat there reading when I heard a sound. There are always sounds in a coal mine even when it is empty and nothing is happening – roof movements, minor falls of dirt, changes in ventilation pressures being the usual culprits and any miner would be familiar with these sounds. I had been an underground worker for twelve years, well aware of my surroundings and the noises and sounds that went with it.

On this day however the sound I heard made me prick my ears. To begin with it was faint, rather distant, but getting nearer. It was the sound of chains rattling. Not the ghostly sound portrayed in films and cartoons but that that might be made by the chain with which a colliery deputy would attach his keys to his belt.

At first I thought the night shift had come on early to do some repair work or prepare for coal cutting on the next shift. Great I thought, this meant I could get out of the pit and go home as a deputy would have come on with the men. I could see myself getting a Friday night pint after all. This was not to be.

After a few seconds I realised that the sound I was hearing was not that of men but of a pit pony making its way to the stables. The chains I could hear rattling were the limmers on its back and I could also hear its hooves as it trotted along the roadway.

This wasn't logical as there hadn't been any ponies at Ireland for over fifteen years. My senses were not deceiving me, I actually heard the sound, a sound not new to me by a long way as I had been a pony driver at Williamthorpe and Holmewood pits during the 1960s.

I listened intently, refusing to believe my own ears but the sound continued to draw ever close. It was beginning to get a little bit scary; the hair on the back of my neck bristled and I started to sweat. I tried to think logically, remembering my training course to be a colliery deputy when I had spent a week at Renishaw Park pit in 1977.

There I had been paired up with deputy Mick Levick and during our conversations the topic of ghosts and the like had cropped up. Mick told me that as a deputy I would sooner or later find myself underground on my own miles away from anyone. His sound advice was that if I thought I saw a ghost I was to keep going forwards towards it and not to turn and run.

The reason for this is simple. If you ran away chances were that from then on you would always be afraid to be on your own in the pit. If you went towards it you might actually discover what it really was – almost always a reflection from your cap lamp.

I thought at the time and still do, that Mick's advice made common sense so I went to the cabin door and looked up and down the roadway. The sound got closer and closer and eventually passed by me. There was nothing to see just the sound of the pony fading into the distance. What struck me later was though I had heard a sound I was familiar with there wasn't the characteristic smell that went with a working horse.

Retreating back into the cabin I whiled away the time trying to make sense of what had occurred. From start to finish the whole experience had lasted a few seconds but it stayed the memory of it will stay with me for the rest of my life and I can tell you that I have never been so pleased in my life to see another human being as when the night turn deputy came on. Over the years I have racked my brain to come up with a proper explanation for the event but I can't find one.

John David Robinson. (Ireland Colliery)

■ Eric Bird (elbow on Anderson Boyes cutter) poses for the camera at Ireland Colliery c1950/51. By 1938 around 60 per cent of British coal was being undercut by electrically operated coal-cutting machinery. (Courtesy Eric Bird)

■ On my eighteenth birthday in 1950 I started training on the coal face at A Winning Colliery and it was at this time that I had to go to the dentist and have four of my front teeth taken out and a small plate put in their place.

At that time we were only allowed fifteen minutes to have our snap so it was a matter of eat it as quickly as possible and then back to the coal face. Well, I couldn't eat with the things so I used to take them out and put them in the lid of my snap tin. At snap time it was also the usual thing to switch your cap lamp onto dim and I had been doing this quite happily for two or three days when something happened. One this particular day I had put my teeth in my snap tin lid and turned my cap lamp to dim as usual and apart from the sound of my mates munching all was quiet. Then, all of a sudden I heard a rattling sound coming from my side, so I put my cap lamp onto full just in time to see a mouse making off with my false teeth. I picked up a stone and threw it at the mouse which dropped my teeth as it made its getaway.

I picked them up, rinsed them off with water from my water bottle and put them back in my mouth. That night I had my first ever date and I daren't have gone to meet her with my front teeth missing.

Stuart Thornley.
A Winning Colliery.

■ A rotating-head roadway cutter loader – better known as a Dosco Roadheader – about to go into action on the Parkgate seam at Bevercotes Colliery on 22 January 1969.

■ Miner Alan Lockley, and his Mk 2 Dosco Roadheader in action at Bevercotes Colliery. (NCB for Sheffield Star special feature on Bevercotes in September 1972)

■ Miners Ces Dronfield and Bill Turner pictured on the face at Bevercotes Colliery. (NCB for Sheffield Star special feature on Bevercotes in September 1972.)

■ And now for something completely different. Creswell Colliery Welfare Band under their conductor Ernest Woodhouse went down the pit on 22 December 1972 and entertained the workforce with a selection of Christmas carols. (Sheffield Star)

■ Tom Hendley,
Face Chargeman at
Creswell Colliery,
February 1978.
(Sheffield Star)

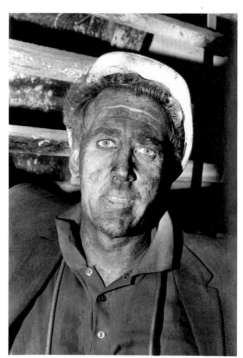

■ This picture was taken on T.1. Unit
Coalface, Markham No.1 Colliery by
D. Buxton. The height of the seam can
be judged by the lamp hanging from
the roof in the middle left background.
(Courtesy D Buxton)

■ Good view of the business end of a Boyes Anderson trepanner; the diameter of the cutting head is 34 in. The main difference between trepanners and shearers is that the trepanner cuts out a cylinder of coal thereby producing large coal, and, as its name suggests, the shearer shears coal off the face thereby producing small coal.

■ Trepanner in action.

By the 1970s the use of timber props at Derbyshire pit faces was a thing of the past and here a power-loader works a prop-free front. To allow up to 6ft 6 in (2 metres) of unsupported roof in front of the hydraulic power supports, the NCB had to win approval of the Mines Inspectorate prior to the concept being introduced. (Derbyshire Times)

■ Preparing for shot firing at Shirebrook.

■ This was the first coalface at Markham No.4 pit not to have stableholds. This means the machine would have to cut all the way into the gateway. As can be seen, the machine is stationed in the gateway waiting for the advanced heading team to allow the face machine to be pushed forward ready for its next journey through the face. The picture shows what a face entry looks like, including one of the two 18ft bearing girders which would support all of the face entry. These would be moved forward in advance, so a section of the archway (the leg) could be extracted in front of the face Crawley, then reset at the back after the turn round. Allowing the machine into the gateway was a great advantage as it allowed fitters and electricians to carry out maintenance work. Andrew Jones, Markham No.4 (NCB official picture)

■ Markham Colliery No.4 bank (bottom deck) as it looked in 1983. (Courtesy Pete Shaw)

■ Markham Colliery No.4 bank (middle deck) and banksman Pete Shaw in 1983. (Courtesy P Shaw)

■ Chair cage, No.4 bank, bottom deck. (Courtesy Pete Shaw)

■ In March 1991 after a "nightmare" nine months, one of Britain's biggest pits was poised to have the best period in its 109-year history thanks to a multi-million pound cash injection.

Central's Markham Colliery was just getting back on its feet after months of heart-ache and frustration with bad ground on both major faces when it was floored again....this time by blizzards which brought the pit to a standstill for almost two full weeks.

The 1,400 men bounced back with a dream start to the New Year, knocking out a regular 50,000tonnes to put the pit back in profit on a week by week basis. And with over £10million being ploughed back into the colliery on new heavy duty tackle and infrastructure, Markham is set to stay in the black.

Leading the revival was the 88s, an advancing panel in the 2m thick Blackshale seam, where cutting teams set a new weekly single face record of 29,063tonnes.

Face overman Mick Hursthouse, who had seen the unit through from day one of its development, said: "The lads have persevered and put in a tremendous effort to work their way through bad ground and weight problems in the main gate which made the stage loader fight. It's now performing better than anyone expected."

The budget-busting performances also lifted Markham's o-m-s to a record level of 6.85tonnes as the pit stepped up a gear on its way to fulfilling its plans to join British Coal's production super league.

Their first big-hitting retreat face in Waterloo seam, 33s, was now coaling, and another heavy duty Waterloo unit was scheduled for June. The £10.4million investment package, that would help the pit improve on its planned output of 1.6million tonnes, included: three sets of heavy duty immediate forward support chocks; three new locomotive systems to replace outdated rope haulages, and three 200-tonne bunkers to improve coal clearance.

Colliery manager Clive Ponder said: "British Coal has shown its faith in Markham's workforce by investing heavily in the pit despite our problems this year."
The Gullick Dobson 4x410 IFS Chocks also proved a real winner with better roof conditions and said Mr Ponder: "Our performances in recent weeks show the investment was a sound one. The return will be even greater in the months ahead because everybody agrees we are set for the best year Markham's ever had."

Markham's record breaking team: back standing, Garry Hollingsworth; middle left to right: Ken Harriss, Tim Gillot, Glynn Power, Dave Smith, John Harper. Front: Steve Clarke and Tony Smith. (Courtesy Glynn Power)

■ No1 Shaft Bolsover Colliery March 1993. Left to right are: Roger Foye, Melvyn Whittaker, Dave Hadfield, Mick Walker and Jim Heath. (Courtesy Mr Whittaker, Chesterfield Local Studies Library)

■ Down darkest Bolsover. (Courtesy David J Higgins)

■ Smiles for the camera. (Courtesy David J Higgins)

ON THE SURFACE

■ This picture was taken at Alfreton Colliery during the 1920s. My grandfather Thomas Spencer is on the front row, fourth from the right. It appears to be a change of shift with those on the right possibly having just emerged from the cage and those on the left being about to go down to start work. This may have been a Derbyshire Times picture as my mother's cousin, Edmund Spencer, was a reporter on your paper, based at Alfreton. (Courtesy Barbara Hobday)

ARKWRIGHT COLLIERY
JOINT PRODUCTION DRIVE
OUTPUT LAST WEEK ... 15621
TARGET OUTPUT ... 14950
GAIN ... + 671

150 YDS

■ Arkwright celebrates beating its weekly target output by 671tonnes. The picture was taken on 25 April 1975. On 26 January 1972 Coal News reported on a visit to the pit by Coalfield Queen, 18-year-old Brenda Cooling, to launch the steepest thin seam in the East Midlands. The new face in the Second E11 had a slope of one in two between gates – as steep as the roof of a house.

Brenda scrambled up the face with only three feet of headroom, and almost straight away bumped into shearer driver Mr Jepson. "Just give the word and we'll cut away enough coal to keep your fire stoked up for the rest of the winter," he told her, pointing to the giant bi-directional 200hp AB shearer, a machine capable of churning out 380tons a shift.

Mr Jepson explained that C20's face – 231 yards from end to end – was the steepest thin seam working in the region, and that the special Dowty steep thin seam supports were the "latest" from the factory.

"Coming up the face is like climbing a ladder," said Brenda. "There's not enough room to swing a pit boot round, so the facemen who got all this equipment set up must have had a really tough job."

Colliery manager Alan Hird said: "Teams on the face are confident they'll be able to make a real go of it once they've got used to the difficult conditions. We're aiming for a face o-m-s of 260cwt – well ahead of the Area average of 198cwt."

As Area director Robert Dunn saw the first load of coal tumble on to the outbye conveyor

■ Former face workers left to right: Kevin Wilcockson, Kevin Marshall, Stephen Brunt and David Pearson pose for the camera at the top of Arkwright Colliery No3 Drift in July 1988. The Colliery officially closed in May/June of that year and miners wishing to stay in the industry were offered employment at other collieries across the region. All four men in the picture had volunteered to Seal Arkwright's four drifts before moving on to employment at other collieries in North Derbyshire.

Stephen Brunt left the industry in late 1989 after a spell at Markham Colliery, going on to take a degree at Sheffield Hallam University then a teaching qualification and finally a Masters Degree from Sheffield University in Post 16 Education and Training. He later worked as a Senior Tutor and Business Development Manager at the Northern College for Adult Education, Barnsley.

■ Arkwright Colliery washery and screens c1989.
(Courtesy Chesterfield Local Studies Library)

■ Bevercotes Colliery, near Worksop, was sunk between 1953 and 1958, this picture being taken in August 1959. It was chosen by the NCB as a test site for advanced mining. By 1976 the Parkgate seam was producing 700,000tonnes a year.

■ Miners hand in their brass checks to the Banksman on coming to the surface.

■ The National Coal Board came into being on 1 January 1947 – known as 'Vesting Day,' thereby bringing the vast majority of coal mines in the United Kingdom into public ownership though a number of small mines – such as Doe Lea Colliery in Derbyshire - remained in private hands.

For administrative purposes the country was divided into divisions. The Scottish Division for Scottish pits; the Northern Division for those in Cumberland, Northumberland and Durham; the North Eastern Division covered Yorkshire; the North Western Division covered North Wales and Lancashire. Collieries in Staffordshire, Shropshire and Warwickshire were grouped into the West Midlands Division whilst Derbyshire's pits found themselves in the East Midlands Division along with collieries in Nottinghamshire and Leicestershire. The South Eastern Division covered the isolated Kent Coalfield and last but by no means least the South Western Division covered South Wales, Gloucestershire and Somerset. This picture was taken at Bolsover on the day. (Courtesy W Skevington)

■ A view of Bolsover Colliery and village taken on 19 November 1981. (Sheffield Star)

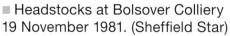

■ Headstocks at Bolsover Colliery
19 November 1981. (Sheffield Star)

■ In November 1985 the NCB
announced changes at the top
at two of North Derbyshire's nine
collieries. Arnold Heeley, manager
at Bolsover since February
1984 was appointed manager at
Markham. His replacement was
Tony Seal (pictured here) who had
been manager at Ireland since
1980. Both had joined the industry
in 1951; Mr Heeley at Glapwell
colliery and Mr Seal at Denby Hall
colliery. (Sheffield Star)

← Full weigh.
← Loco shed.
← Winding house.
← Washery.
← Materials yard.

← EMERGENCY WINDER ROUTE

■ This picture was taken on 22 October 1985 and published three days later in the Sheffield Star for a feature covering the last shift at Brookhouse Colliery. (Sheffield Star)

■ Brookhouse Colliery
on 22 October 1985.
(Sheffield Star)

■ Coal screening at Clay Cross. It might not look it but this work was
backbreaking yet in Edwardian times it was considered suitable employment
for older workers or those who had been injured. The picture was originally
published as a postcard (No105) by the Clay Cross Colliery Co.

■ Screening coal at Creswell Colliery. Derbyshire Times reader Stuart Thornley wrote of his experience on the screen when he started working at A Winning Colliery in 1948. For the first three months I worked on the pit top at what was then called bat scratching. The coal came up the pit on a large metal conveyor belt and my job was to pick the dirt (bats) out of the coal. It could be a back-breaking, dirty job, especially on a Monday morning when there was more than just bats and coal on the belt. The only toilet down the mine was one at the pit bottom which wasn't much use to you when you were probably two miles away and had had a good weekend on the beer.

■ Dinnington Main Colliery was originally projected by the Sheffield Coal Company in 1899 but the development costs associated with sinking a deep pit were such that they were forced to look for a business partner which they found in the form of the Sheepbridge Coal & Iron Co. Sinking finally commenced during 1902, coal being struck in 1904. (Sheffield Star)

■ NCB Chairman Sir Derek Ezra (centre) pays a visit to Dinnington Main in August 1979. With him are NCB South Yorkshire Director Geoff Hayes (left) and colliery manager Jo Armishaw (right) (Sheffield Star)

■ The colliery tip at Dinnington had already been an eyesore for years when David Vaughan turned up in early June 1975 to take this image for the Morning Telegraph. Plans had been announced to reduce the height of the tip and landscape it; phase-one had already begun. The picture was taken in Plantation Street. (Morning Telegraph)

■ It is June 1955 and the NCB is in the process of modernising Glapwell Colliery. The picture, taken from Stockley Lane, shows the Bramley Vale No1 Drift under construction. (Courtesy Chesterfield Local Studies Library)

■ Here we travel back in time with these two images showing Grassmoor Colliery's Humbolt Washery under construction was taken on 30 May 1899. Grassmoor was the first colliery in the county to install pit head baths which were officially opened in December 1929 by the then Minister of Mines, Ben Turner. They were erected under the Miners' Welfare Scheme at a cost of about £15,000. The scheme provided the money the company gave the land, water and fuel. Miners had 2d a week deducted from their pay towards the cost of maintenance. (Courtesy Chesterfield Local Studies Library)

■ Haworth Colliery as it looked in August 1967. On Vesting Day, Harworth was assigned to the NCB's East Midland Division, Area No.3. The reorganisation of March 1967 placed it in the newly created North Nottinghamshire Area. From 1990 further reorganisations due to the massive rundown the industry put the pit in the Nottinghamshire Area (1 April 1990) and later in the Midlands Group (1 September 1993). Under privatisation the colliery passed to RJB Mining on 30 December 1994. (Sheffield Star)

■ Members of the Blyth Parent Teachers association at Harworth Colliery near Worksop after a Sunday morning tour of the underground workings in March 1976. (Sheffield Star)

■ In December 2003, UK Coal announced that Harworth would share in a Government Investment Aid package totalling £36.5million to access coal reserves. £4.6million would go towards projects including a new 320-metre long retreat face and driving 6000 metres of underground roadways to access 8million tonnes. (Sheffield Star)

■ Hartington Colliery was situated between Staveley and Renishaw, closing in 1930. Hartington later provided Upcast and emergency egress for Ireland Colliery as well as some limited manriding capability. It was also the site of Ireland's major pumping installation.

■ Ireland was the first major colliery to be sunk in the Markham Valley. For nearly 75 years the colliery's output came from the Deep Soft seam and it was not until after nationalisation that production of Deep Hard commenced.

■ Ireland Colliery. In November 1991 councillors were opposing plans for a 121-acre opencast site in the Netherthorpe area of Staveley. The project to extract 328,000 tonnes of coal included diverting the heavily polluted River Doe Lea and digging up agricultural land, wetland areas, and two former Ireland Colliery tips. Staveley Town Council was also opposed to the scheme, claiming it would create traffic hazards and that the site was too close to recent housing developments and Netherthorpe School. Fitzwise Ltd, the company behind the scheme, told the Derbyshire Times that: "The scheme would help safeguard 40 people's jobs for at least 18 months but it wouldn't create any new jobs."
(Courtesy W Skevington)

■ Changing winding wheels at Ireland colliery. (Courtesy J Ward)

■ The colliery yard at Langwith. (Courtesy W. Skevington)

■ Langwith Colliery wages department make a visit underground in the picture taken around 1960. Left to right are: Alf Trolley (Training Officer), Ernest Clarke (Chief Clerk), Ron Allsop, Malcolm Garland, Ron Holland, Dorothy Harris, Eileen Rhodes, Eli Harris, Olive Allcott, Philip Utridge, Hazel Shirtcliffe and Jack Roberts (Safety Officer). (Courtesy Philip Utridge)

■ A pay day at Langwith Colliery c1960; Malcolm Garland is dishing out the dosh and Alan Collier riding shotgun in the background. (Courtesy Philip Utridge)

■ Lunchtime at Langwith and Ron Allsop deals off the top to Olive Allcott. (Courtesy Philip Utridge)

■ It was not until the late 1970s that the last of the NCB's own electricity networks were discontinued and power was taken from the East Midland's Electricity Board. Indeed in 1951 no less than 20 collieries in North Derbyshire and North Nottinghamshire not only had their own generation but a number were also supplying power to nearby villages. This was often supplied at a fixed weekly price per household, mine employees having the money stopped automatically from their pay. Shirebrook had one of the more eccentric systems in that every house was fitted with a flicker switch. If the householder attempted to have more than three 60watt lights on at the same time, the flicker switch would kick in and flick the lights off and on until the load was reduced.

■ Students on the NCB mechanical apprentices advanced course at Duckmanton Workshops in 1963. (Courtesy Chesterfield Local Studies Library)

■ By 1975 Markham colliery was running five separate seams and was one of the largest pits in the country. From August that year Markham began winding coal from the connected Ireland Colliery for which it also provided official second egress. The view is of the colliery Area workshops and the No2 end of the yard. (Courtesy Chesterfield Local Studies Library)

■ No 1 and No 4 headstocks at Markham Colliery in 1983. The combined saleable output from Markham and Ireland was now over 2 million tonnies a year. Six seams were in production through the Deep Soft, Deep Hard and First Piper were close to exhaustion. (Courtesy Pete Shaw)

■ The clutter in Markham stockyard in June 1987. Still operational at the start of the 1990s Markham was one of Derbyshire's last three collieries to close, shutting in 1993 together with Bolsover and Shirebrook.

■ Pleasley Colliery situated some 8 miles east of Chesterfield, was originally owned by the Stanton Ironworks Company and went into production in the early 1870s. The pit closed in 1983 but escaped the wholesale demolition visited upon other collieries with headstocks, engine houses and steam winders surviving. The old colliery was chosen to be the focal point of a country park and restoration of the spoil heaps begain in the 1990s. (Courtesy W Skevington)

■ Parkhouse Colliery at play at the Derbyshire Miners' Holiday Camp, Skegness, in the summer of 1952. Standing left to right are: Jim Sutton, George Spencer, Colin Holmes, George Holmes, George Bradley, Dennis Fellows, Dennis Lawrence, Ken Holmes, Dennis Lunn, and George Findley. Seated left to right are: Geoff Wainwright, Dickie Sutton, George Muldoon, Stan Kirk, Keith Pettit, and Glynn Griffiths. (Courtesy George Holmes)

■ The guys at Pleasley Colliery take a break from their joint production drive to pose for posterity. Power-loading came to Pleasley in late 1946 with the installation of a Huwood ML/1 on a long wall face in the Deep Hard seam. Despite some teething problems, the ML/1 proved its worth and within a few years these machines were responsible for 90 per cent of Deep Hard output. The Huwood loaders were popular because their small overall dimensions (only 6ft 4 in high by 2ft 10 in wide) meant there was no need to blast out large stable holes; indeed one report on Pleasley states that the operators had become so adept that practically no blasted coal from the stable hold had to be hand loaded.

Alas the pit would be the first in the county to be closed in the 1980s, going in 1983. Westhorpe followed in 1984, and from the end of the 1984-85 strike to the end of the decade the county lost a further eight pits. Measham and Whitwell in 1986; Ireland in 1987; Cadley Hill and Arkwright in 1988; Rawdon, Renishaw Park and Warsop in 1989. (Sheffield Star)

SHIREBROOK COLLIERY.

■ My father was a miner at Shirebrook and in the late 1920s we lived in a terraced house in the now demolished Market Street. Two bedrooms, kitchen, living room, front room, outside toilet, gas lighting, black stove, and no running hot water.

At the time my dad worked three days on, three days off, and on Mondays – one of his off days – we often went to Mansfield on the train to have a look round the market, my childhood memories of which are puppies and kittens for sale, mushy peas, and cockles and whelks(ugh!).

Shirebrook had a Friday market and there seemed to be stalls and shops all the way from the railway station to the Market Place which was also the venue for the annual visit of the fun fair.

During the thirties dad acquired an allotment which meant we could grow most of our own vegetables and we also kept a few hens for eggs. No one in their right mind ate a hen until its egg producing days were over. One of our neighbours, Reggie Brewster, kept pigs and any food waste we had went to Reggie to help feed them. Every Christmas Reggie would kill a pig and give us a joint.

In those days the majority of miners' wives made their own bread; an old deaf and dumb man went from house to house selling yeast out of a great cane basket he carried on his arm. Milk was delivered by a horse-drawn cart and served fresh from a churn.
It was during the thirties that we moved to a flat up by the allotments; still no running hot water, still lit by gaslight, still with an outside loo. On washdays my mother boiled up the water in a copper. By this time she was a midwife and her white uniform was immaculate. I know I learned to iron her apron pleats using out two flat irons warmed on the gas ring. (Mrs Cynthia Robinson, nee Quenby)

■This picture was taken on our allotment at Shirebrook. The miners' allocation of coal was trundled down from the colliery to the 'Coal Wharf' in the background. The trucks were unloaded by hand and the coal was delivered to miners' homes by horse-drawn cart. Our coal was tipped on the 'backs' and dad had to shovel it into the coalhouse at the bottom of the steps to our flat. (Courtesy Mrs Cynthia Robinson nee Quenby)

■ A superb image of Shirebrook Colliery taken by Roger Grayson.

■The deputy and the lampman

■ Warsop Main Colliery viewed from the main access road. No2 shaft is nearest the camera.

■ Welbeck Colliery celebrates its first 1millionth tonne in a year.

WELBECK COLLIERY
1,000,000 TONNES
13-11-90

■ Welbeck Colliery was in the news on 24 February 2005 following a deal being struck to keep the loss-making pit open for a few more years. Only two weeks earlier, UK Coal had announced the pit's closure due to 'geological problems' and falling profits. Miners agreed to work longer but fewer shifts that would see a 40 per cent increase in the hours pit machinery would be in operation; up from 100 to 140 hours a week.

■ This picture of Pie Bank and the Gantry at Williamthorpe Colliery was taken prior to the pit's modernisation programme of 1938-40. (Courtesy Chesterfield Local Studies Library)

■ Officials of the Hardwick Colliery Company and invited guests appear incapable of raising a smile for the camera at the opening of the pithead baths at Williamthorpe Colliery in 1941. (Courtesy Chesterfield Local Studies Library)

■ Somewhere in deepest Derbyshire in January 1941, this 100-acre wood was being turned into pit-props for 20 local collieries. (Derbyshire Times)

■ During the Second World War, a number of opencast were brought into use in Derbyshire, many on a short term basis as an essential contribution to the nation's fuel supply. As the coal at the majority of these sites was near the surface, and the method used to extract it was simple. First, bulldozers removed the topsoil to expose the coal and this was the dug out by excavators. By August 1944, when this picture was taken, some sites had been exhausted and work was already underway to restore the land to its former use for agricultural purposes. (Derbyshire Times)

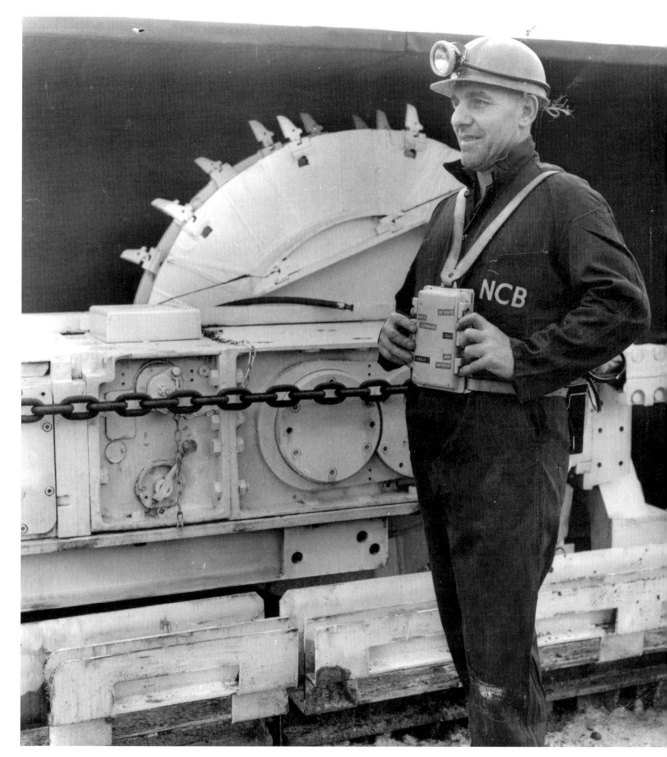

■ In the mid-1960s this shearing machine was experimentally fitted for remote operation. It is pictured here on the surface being operated for the benefit of the Press. Though the picture was taken at neither a Derbyshire, nor a Nottinghamshire pit, it has been included to show some of the kit the NCB was playing around with at the time. A machine of this type was deployed at Hatfield Main Colliery, Yorkshire, by October 1967. (Sheffield Star)

■ Dosco roadheading machines come in all shapes and sizes, the largest weighing in at over 100 tonnes. This picture taken in the mid-1980s shows a Dosco undergoing clearance tests.

■ The NCB invited members of the Press to inspect the latest in longwall mining equipment prior to it being taken down pit. The business part of the unit – the coal cutting machine – is in the middle of the picture and is linked to a chain drive disappearing off at bottom right. The cutter is sitting over the trough of an armoured face conveyor (AFC). Made of steel sections loosely linked together so they can be snaked sideways or in a curve, the

AFC runs the length of the face. As coal falls into the trough it is moved along the AFC by means of paddles attached to endless chains – four paddles can be seen in this image – and discharged to the roadway transport system.

■ Members of Chesterfield Mining Society on a visit to Victor Products in March 1961. Most of these men went of to become senior management in the NCB. (Courtesy D Burton)

■ Members of year III of the Derbyshire NUM day release course held at Hurst House, December, 1988. Back row left to right: Gary Whitehead, Steve Beardmore, Brett Shaw, Ian Proffit, Dave Taylor. Front row: Ian Cooke, George Hampson, Clive Bowater, Mall Abbott and Glynn Power. (Courtesy Glynn Power)

■ If asked to describe a coal mine, the majority of use would come up with a large complex with headstocks employing hundreds of men. Few of us would come up with a footrail – usually pronounced footrill – and invariably a small drift mine employing perhaps a few dozen men at most. Well, Derbyshire had its fair share of footrails and this is what our reader D Robotham had to say about them.

"Around 1900 my great great grandfather Henry Lowton, owned a colliery at Lowgates in Staveley called the Wagon Main Footrill - usually pronounced "Wang-em." Apparently the mine never made any money; unlike his other business, a tripe shop in Staveley. In fact the shop was so prosperous that one of his sons, Arthur – who worked underground - wanted a slice of the action. When Henry refused Arthur ran amok. He shot and killed his mother then turned the gun on himself to commit suicide. He failed. Arthur was tried and condemned to death but managed to cheat the hangman by dying of his wounds in Chesterfield Royal Hospital". The picture was taken in about 1900 and shows Arthur Lowton, Fred Hobson and Elijah Rush. Rush was later killed down Hartington Colliery. (Courtesy D. Robotham)

■ This second picture supplied by Mr Robotham shows members of the Lowton family at Wang-em Main around 1902. Included are Arthur Lowton (left) with Ernest, John and Frank in the middle. (Courtesy D. Robotham)

■ Its eyes down, look in as the 1000th mine shaft to be capped in Derbyshire was officially performed on Bonsall Moor, near Matlock, on 23 June 1980, by the Chairman of the Public Protection Committee for Derbyshire Councillor Arthur Stretton (wearing helmet). It must be pointed out that these were by no means all coal mine shafts; hundreds were former lead or fluorspar workings. The actual number of abandoned mine workings in the county is still unknown as new ones are being discovered all the time. There was a case a few years ago of someone's lounge suddenly disappearing when a big hole opened up underneath it. The house had been built over an abandoned shaft which had been capped with timber but the timber had rotted away. (Derbyshire Times)

ON THE MOVE

■ Pit bottom at Clay Cross and tubs full of CXC Gold Medal coal are being manhandled into the cage for hauling up. This image is taken from postcard No119 in the Clay Cross series.

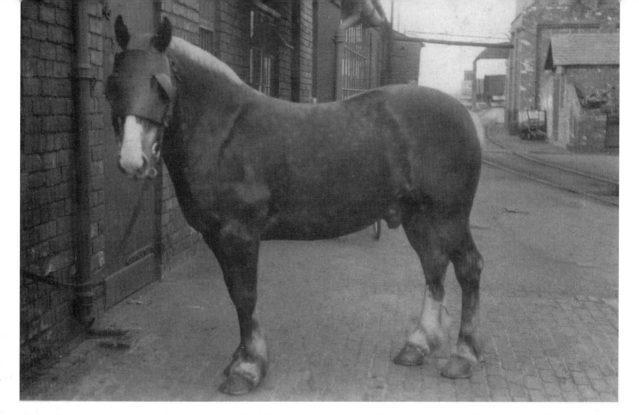

■This picture supplied by Derbyshire Times reader Richard J Adam shows one of Ireland Colliery's pit ponies. Ponies continued to be used in some North Derbyshire pits well into the 1960s and another reader, Stuart Thornley, has sent the following account of his time as a pony driver at A Winning Colliery.

As soon as you reached sixteen years-of-age you were allowed underground though the first couple of weeks or so was spent working in the pit bottom. One Monday morning the pit bottom corporal shouted, "Thornley, goo int' stables an' gerra hoss." So off I went not really knowing what to expect. By that time there were only half a dozen horses left at A Winning; once there had been twenty-six.

Abe Beers from South Normanton was the ostler. He took me to the back of this horse, which wasn't a pony I can tell you. Abe said, "Here thar are, Butes his name, thar'll be orate wi' him, ayes blind in one eye but knows where to goo." The deputy went with me to show me the way to the main gate in the three-quarter seam in the Law Main. My job was to load bar that had been straightened on the bar press and then go over the overcast into the tail gate, where they would be put on the coalface belt to be used again.
Although Bute was a big horse, he was gentle and after a few weeks we became a great team. At that time new leaf was just coming on the hawthorne bushes and I would take him some everyday.

We had been working together for about four months when one day Bute didn't seem to be himself. He was very nervous and constantly shaking his head and when we set off he travelled faster than normal down the tailgate. I stopped him and when I unhitched him from the jotty of bars he walked forward and straight into the bip end.

"Wots up wi 'im!" shouted timber man Joe Holmes. Joe took off his cap lamp and shone it into Bute's good eye. Bute never flinched. "Ayes gone blind altogether; we'd better send for Billy Wall."

Billy Wall was the deputy out of Main Gate. He looked over Bute "Arr he's blind alright, tek 'im back t'stables."

So here I was, a lad of sixteen two miles out from the pit bottom with a totally blind horse. We set off. I talked to Bute the whole time as we made our way along. The first half mile or so was okay: then we came to a swilly, a dip in the roadway where the endless haulage rope stands about two feet off the ground. As Bute straddled the rope I could see it was only just under his belly but as it was nearing the end of the shift I thought no one would switch the haulage rope on. I was wrong. The rope suddenly whirred into life and hit Bute and he reared up. I tried to hang onto him in the hope that some of the men on the afternoon shift would soon turn up but had to let go when he took off at breakneck speed. He must have been very frightened. I set off after him but stopped shortly afterwards when I came across a cloud of coal dust. I couldn't see a thing at first but as it cleared I began to inch my way forward till I came to a junction. Being blind poor old Bute had galloped straight into an upright steel girder. He was dead.

I didn't know what to do I just stayed there with him until the twinkling of lights coming towards me. It was the afternoon shift. Before long someone had shoved a tub along the track and the men had packed old Bute into it like a sardine in a tin. A slip was put on the haulage rope and off Bute went to the knacker's yard.

What I never understood was that they didn't ask me what had happened and when I turned up for work the following morning I wasn't asked any questions by the management. The only thing anyone said was when I got down to the pit bottom and that was "Goo into stables an' gerra nother oss."

I suppose that was life down pit in 1948.

■ Ostler William Arthur Hinchcliffe and Vic, one of the ponies he cared for, at the underground stables at Ireland Colliery. (Courtesy Richard J Adams)

■ Samuel Wilfred Hinchliffe and Snap pictured together on College Avenue, Staveley in 1924. Samuel and Snap had landed first prize in the local Wakes Week pony driving competition. (Courtesy Richard J Adams)

"Snap" - 1st Prize (1924) - S.W. Hinchcliffe.

■ Ireland Colliery ponies and drivers pose for the camera on College Avenue, Staveley. Arthur William Hinchcliffe is second from the left and to his left stand Walter Goodwin, Samuel Arthur Hinchcliffe and Len Brownlow. (Courtesy Richard J Adam)

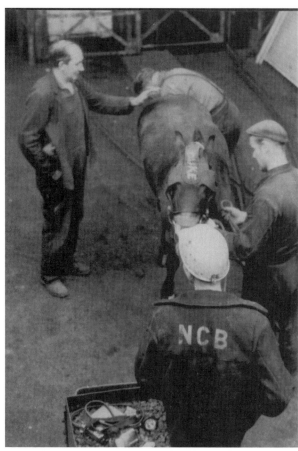

■ The last of Ireland Colliery's pit ponies were retired in 1970. (Courtesy J Ward)

■ Billy the gang pony at South Normanton Colliery was already 26 years old when this picture was taken around 1909-10 Billy had worked at the colliery for 24 years.

■ Opening in 1795 and closing in 1908, the Little Eaton Gangway was built to carry coal from Denby Hall, Salterwood North, and Henmoor collieries to a branch of the Derby Canal at Little Eaton. As the Gangway also served Denby Potteries and Smithy Houses it also carried general freight including pottery, stone, and timber. A gang consisted of a driver, team of four horses harnessed in single file and eight wagons.

The 'main line' was four miles long and it was then another mile to Denby Hall Colliery; the carter having to walk at the head of the lead horse.

As can be seen in this picture the track is made of lengths of L-shape iron plates laid on oak sleepers. One advantage of this type of track was that the wagons could still run even if it was out of gauge by an inch or two.

And, if you think the containerisation of goods is relatively new then think again because the method was employed on the Gangway from the very beginning.
(Courtesy Clive Hardy)

■ There were three types of wagons on the Gangway each consisting of a chassis (the tram) and a body (the box). The main wagon type was able to carry around 48cwt of coal. A second type had slated sides and was used for carrying stone; a third type was used for general goods traffic. At the canal wharf the boxes were lifted off the trams by crane and lowered directly into the waiting narrowboat for onward shipment to Derby. In the previous picture you can see a box has been lifted clear of its tram for loading. Horses considered too old to work in the gangs were employed shunting wagons around the wharf. This picture of a Gangway coal wagon was taken at the Midland Railway Centre, Butterley. (Courtesy Clive Hardy)

■ The Midland Railway's Doe Lea branch line linked Bolsover, Glapwell and Pleasley. This is Glapwell in the days when it was owned by the Sheepbridge Coal & Iron Company. The Midland Railway station can be seen at right with the colliery's busy sidings over to the left; the pit was busy enough to have a roster of three shunting engines. (Courtesy W Skevington)

■ Shipley Colliery Company mine workers head for home aboard their local 'Paddy Mail' a colloquial term for a colliers' work train. Many collieries were served by such trains, usually comprised of elderly passenger vehicles rather than open coal wagons and running over distances of between two and ten miles. That this train has a coal wagon full of miners nailed to its rear suggests that it will not be going too far though it looks as though it had running rights for a short distance over Midland Railway tracks. There were a number of these trains running in the Chesterfield area such as one to Glapwell which was introduced in September 1886 but operated by the Midland Railway Co. Another service introduced by the Midland was on the Ramcroft branch in September 1918 though it was withdrawn in October 1927. The Glapwell Paddy ceased operating in September 1931. This picture, taken in Edwardian times was published as a postcard in the Peveril Series.

■ On the move to the 1924 British Empire Exhibition, Wembley Park, was this lump of coal weighing nearly three tonnes mined by hand at Markham Colliery by two brothers named Smith who came from Newbold. (Courtesy Derrick Frearson)

■ Chosen as the standard shunting engine for the Ministry of Supply in World War Two the 'Austerity' 0-6-0 saddle tank turned out to be one of the UK's most successful designs for a steam shunting locomotive. To save time, the design was based on an existing model built by the Hunslet Engine Company; to save money and materials a leaf was taken out of the Victory ship building programme. Welded assemblies were used wherever practical such as the cab, coal bunker, saddle water tank, and main frames, and the main visual difference between old and new design was that here the saddle tank was extended over the top of the smokebox.

The Ministry of Supply's order for nearly 400 of these robust and powerful engines was split between several commercial locomotive manufacturers. After the war the MoS sold 75 of these engines to the London & North Eastern Railway as well as large numbers to the NCB, British Steel and so on. So successful was the design that new locomotives, albeit with modifications, continued to be built into the 1960s.

The Austerity 0-6-0 saddle tanks were the operational steam engines employed by the NCB and ironically the last survivor of the former LNER engines in service with British Railways (No. 68012) was transferred to Westhouses engine shed in May 1967 to work at Williamthorpe Colliery.

Our picture, taken at Coppice Colliery, Ilkeston, shows former MoS No.75035; built by the Hunslet Engine Co in 1943 and purchased by the NCB East Midlands Division in 1947. (Courtesy Vic Hall)

■ British Railway's 0-6-0 tank engine No 47629 shunting at Wiliamthorpe Colliery. Over 400 of these locomotives were built between 1924 and 1930 becoming the standard shunting tank engine of the London Midland & Scottish Railway. The first of the class to be withdrawn was No 47331 in April 1959; the last Nos 47289 and 47629 based at Westhouses engine shed for shunting at Williamthorpe Colliery, were withdrawn in October 1967. (Courtesy W Skevington)

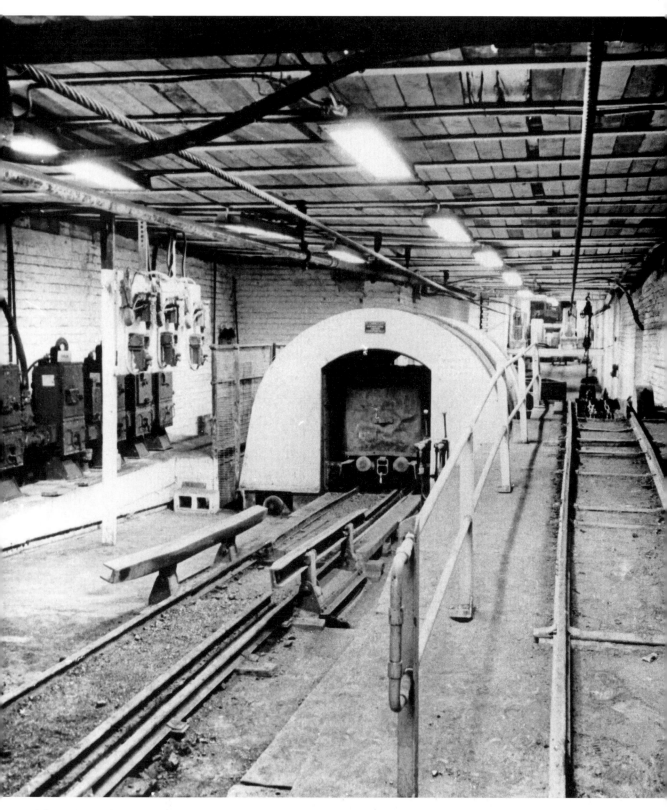

■ View from East Plane top of the 3-tub tipper and new 400hp haulage at Glapwell Colliery. (Courtesy Chesterfield Local Studies Library)

A 'coolie car' unit carrying rails for extending the track turns a right angle bend in a roadway at Alfreton Colliery. The picture, taken on 15 September 1964, clearly shows the continuous haulage rope running between the rails. (Sheffield Star)

Not a ride at Alton Towers but a rope haulage manrider at Creswell Colliery.

■ Though usually employed underground, some collieries also used their flameproof mines locomotives on the surface to work the stockyards. On 28 September 1944, the commercial locomotive manufacture Hudswell Clarke & Co teamed up with Hugh Wood Mining to build and market flameproof mines locomotives. By no means first in the field to build this type of locomotive, the partnership was determined to be the first to produce a 100hp machine capable of passing the exacting tests required to obtain a certificate that would enable it to work in any colliery in the UK.

The 100hp Huwood-Hudswell was a 0-6-0 fitted with a Gardner 6LW engine. Transmission was through Vulcan Sinclair scoop controlled fluid couplings to a Synclair syncro-self-shifting powerflow three-speed gearbox, a sophisticated drive, yet easily operated. On changing gear upwards, the drive was maintained thereby preventing any snatching at the drawbar. The prototype was delivered for trials to Moorgreen Colliery, Nottinghamshire, in October 1946.

A 68p 0-4-0 variant appeared in 1947, followed by a 25hp chain driven model in 1951. Also in 1951 came the first 200hp machine; simply two 100hp units capable of being controlled from one cab. They could also be split and used as individual locomotives

■ A flameproof mines locomotive in its underground garage. (Courtesy Clive Hardy)

■ A manrider train on the 2ft 4in gauge underground system at Bevercotes Colliery. A surface narrow gauge locomotive was used in the stockyard during the construction period; the underground system becoming operational during 1965.

■Taken in 1983, this picture shows a GMT (Gyro Mining Transport) manriding set in use at Markham No2 Colliery. No3 and No2 headstocks are in the background. (Courtesy Pete Shaw)

■ Manriders came in all shapes and sizes and did not always involve a train. In some collieries men travelled to and from the face by conveyor belt. At Babbington Colliery, Nottinghamshire, miners went to and from the face in individual chairs slung beneath a monorail and anyone not in the know would have been forgiven for thinking the entire system had been bought second hand from a Swiss ski resort. The manrider unit pictured here was built be Clayton Equipment, Hatton.

■ In January 1992, six overhead wire electric flameproofed locomotives were transferred from Gedling Colliery for use on the proposed 3ft gauge underground system at Harworth. However the project was cancelled and the locomotives sent to the Clayton Equipment Co.

■ When this picture was taken at Bevercotes Colliery in July 1965, the pit was scheduled to be producing 1.5million tonnes of coal a year by 1968 from five remotely-operated coal faces and with a labour force of 770 men.

The central control room at the pithead managed underground transport, winding, coal preparation plant, surface and underground ancillary operations. The image shows the main west trunk conveyor drivehead station, looking inbye. (NCB for Sheffield Star special feature on Bevercotes)

■ Rail-mounted power pack for face operations at Bevercotes. (NCB for Sheffield Star special feature on Bevercotes)

■ The control room at Bevercotes

■ The merry-go-round (mgr) train concept was introduced to provide the CEGB's new generation of coal-fired power stations including Drax, Cottam, Didcot, Ferrybridge and Willington, with a constant supply of coal. A number of older collieries were re-equipped with rapid loading systems enabling trains of thirty or more wagons to be loaded in less than one hour. The first of these facilities to become operational was at Langwith Colliery, whilst new collieries such as Bevercotes came on line with the system installed. On arrival at the mgr equipped power station, the train would take a circular route at slow speed through the complex, each wagon being unloaded automatically through its bottom discharge doors as it passed over the hopper conveyor system. To operate the service BR invested in a fleet of high capacity 32-tonne payload, air-braked wagons, and a number of locomotives were fitted with Slow Speed Control (SSC) enabling them to run at a constant half-mile-per-hour when loading/discharging operations were in progress. The picture shows a mgr train loading at Bevercotes with 1000 tonnes of coal for Trentside power station.

One outcome of the 1984-85 strike was the decision by the CEGB to switch to road transport. Traditionally, power station coal from collieries such as Bolsover had gone by rail, but during the strike deliveries had been temporarily switched to road because the rail unions had supported the NUM.

■ The newly installed merry-go-round loading facility at Shirebrook prior to full commissioning.

■ In December 1982 BR invited the Press to Doncaster Works for the official unveiling of the first of the new Class 58 diesel-electric locomotives. With a maximum power output of 3300hp, these locomotives were capable of hauling the heaviest mgr coal trains single-handedly whereas some of BR's older types had either had to work in multiple or be assisted for part of their journey. For example the Class 47 locomotives operating out of Worksop needed assistance as far as Dinnington.

■ Steam winding engines were often kept in immaculate condition by their enginemen. (Sheffield Star)

No.4 WINDING ENGINE HOUSE.

■ Markham No.4 winding engine house control room with engineman David Owen in command. The pictures were taken in 1993. (Courtesy John Barry Keyworth)

■ One of the large dump trucks used at Renishaw Pit. On occasion spoil and waste was put to use. In the late 1960s waste from Bolsover was used to partially fill one of the tunnels on the former Lancashire Derbyshire & East Coast line, while during the 1970s Duckmanton Tunnel was filled with waste from Arkwright. (Courtesy A Price)

■ A NCB lorry delivers coal to miners' homes around Warsop Vale. Though the colliery was producing coal by 1898 work on providing homes for miners did not get underway until 1900; the Staveley Coal & Iron Co paying the builder £40 for each dwelling. The three-bedroom houses were built in rows of terraces each of eight, ten or twelve dwellings on three sides of a square, the colliery being on the fourth.

ACCIDENTS & DISASTERS

■ The history of mining is littered with accidents and disasters and local pits had their fair share and to include them all would make a book in its own right. In December 1926 there was a shaft accident at Williamthorpe Colliery, in which eight men were injured. The cage was dashed into the bottom when it should have been raised.

On 9 April 1951 a Meco-Moore cutting and power-loading machine and its seven man crew were buried under a roof fall at Denby Hall Colliery, Ripley. The fall came without warning completely burying five men and partially burying the other two. The two partially buried miners were soon released and taken to the Derbyshire Royal Infirmary where they were found to have only minor injuries. The condition of the roof was such that rescuers had to work slowly to free the remaining five. Speaking in the House of Commons on 10 April, the Minister for Fuel, Mr Philip Noel-Baker said: "The dangerous condition of the roof hampered the efforts to extricate the other men, but the rescue squads have so far recovered the bodies of two of the remaining five, one at 4.30 and the other at 7.30 this morning.

"The rescue work is going on, but to my deep regret there now seems to be little hope that any of the other men can be alive. I am sure the House would wish me to express their gratitude to the rescue squads, who have been working in perilous conditions and their deep sympathy with the families and friends of the miners who have lost their lives." Even though the industry is now only a shadow of its former self, accidents still happen.

At Welbeck in November 2007, a miner with 27 years experience in the industry at Pleasley, Shirebrook, Clipstone, and Harworth collieries, died of injuries received from a fall when rock flushed from the coalface's roof after a hydraulic support was lowered during a routine operation.

RAILWAY SMASH CHESTERFIELD

■ The wreck of the Grassmoor Colliery "Paddy Mail" was front page news in the Derbyshire Times on 15 September 1906, and what follows is an edited version of the page. "The Paddy Mail" – the familiar name in colliery districts for the workmen's train – is almost a household word in an area like Chesterfield. Every day, morning and evening, hundreds – indeed thousands – of men who work underground are conveyed to and from their work over distances ranging from two to perhaps ten miles. Knowing this, as residents of Chesterfield district do, a natural dread descended upon Chesterfield and district that Tuesday morning, when news went round that the Grassmoor "mail" on the Midland Railway had met with disaster near Tapton. Early as is was, many people crowded towards the railway bridge on the Brimington Road from which they could view the site of the collision.

The train to which the mishap occurred was transporting the miners from Dronfield, Unstone, Sheepbridge and Chesterfield to the Grassmoor Collieries, with some of the men joining the Glapwell "mail" at Chesterfield. At the same time, an engine arrived at Tapton Junction from Staveley, with the object of taking out a ballast train which stood in its own siding on the west side of the main lines. From Staveley it arrived on the goods line and in order to reach the ballast siding, it had to cross over the main passenger lines. The driver, Sam Machin, and the fireman, Dixon, of Staveley, in making the move, got over the down passenger line but found the "dummy" – as the signal is called – against them, and so remained with the engine on the up line, almost under the bridge which carries the Chesterfield and Brimington Road over the railway. Thus, the ballast engine stood right in the track of the "mail" for which the signals were clear.

Although it was travelling at a relatively slow speed due to heavy fog, the driver on the workmen's train, Joe Williams, heard no fog detonator and so proceeded on his way, quite unaware of the presence of the locomotive near the bridge into which the tender of his engine, which was travelling backwards, then crashed. The force of the collision derailed both engines and the first coach of the twelve comprising the workmen's train. A sudden stop, and then the "mail" engine scraped forward dragging the derailed coach with it. The weight of the other carriages on the first carriage caused it to rear up against the engine, and the sight of its wheels over the funnel of the locomotive met those who were first arrived on the scene.

■ Taken at the Chesterfield Mines Rescue Station, Fords Colliery No1 Rescue Team from Marehay Colliery, Ripley, take a break during a training exercise. The question is: Was the dog a team member? The 1911 Coal Mines Act laid down standards for mines rescue stations; equipment, training, codes of practice. The stations were to be funded by the Colliery Owners Association.

■ Dated 18 October 1930, though it could be earlier, this picture of the head stock at Beighton Colliery (Brookhouse) accompanied a Sheffield Telegraph article about an accident in which one miner had been killed and ten others injured. There was an overwind accident at Brookhouse in 1958 when a new electric winding system on the miners' shaft cage broke and 36 men were seriously injured when the cage went out of control. The injured were brought out by stretcher up a steep incline of about a mile in length to the Beighton shaft.
(Morning Telegraph)

Markham 1938

Derbyshire Times reader, Olwyne Moore, provided us with part of a 1998 school project completed by Caroline Moore, which included an account of her grandfather Charles Alwyne Moore's involvement in the 1938 Markham pit disaster.

"My name is Charles Alwyne Moore, I am now almost 91 years old but at the time of the disaster 1 was only 30 years old and working as a deputy down No.2 Mine.

On the day of the explosion, I had not long started my shift down No.2 Mine when they rang down form the pit head and called me and other colliery officials to the surface. As I approached the surface I could hear the sirens sounding; I had to draw a fresh lamp and go down the Blackshale.

I was with a man called Bert Wall, and we were told by Mr Whitehouse to put up Fastcloth in the Main Gate and either side of the crossing to stop the ventilation and not let anybody past till the rescue teams arrived.

They sent down stretcher bearers and I had to load the dead miners onto the stretchers and place the lamp that was nearest to each miner between their feet for identification purposes.

The first six men I loaded up had been at the entrance to the Gate and had received terrible injuries. The next two men were just around the corner off the Main Roadway, sitting with their backs to a pack as if they were resting. These two and another four men had been killed by carbon monoxide poisoning.

I was eventually told to go up the pit and go home and rest.

The next day I went into work. As I had spent some time in the past working in the Blackshale, and I knew the area well, the overman, Wilf Brooks, told me I was to spend the next week taking Mines Inspectors and people form ICI and Nobell explosive manufacturers around for them to see what had happened.

At the bottom of 2 Unit, four of the supporting rings had been blown over into one another and on the face all of the roof supports had been blown out. At 2 Unit Main Gate Ripping Lip, the explosion had picked up a tub full of stone and turned it upside down with the stone still in it. In the Lip, there were charges of powder with detonators in place, which we had to recover. We also searched for and found some 3 and 4 ounce charges of unused powder which had been stashed behind packs at the side of the roadway.

Soon after being involved in this disaster, I myself joined the official underground mines rescue team, but was fortunate never again to be called to anything as devastating as the Markham No.1 Colliery explosion of 10 May 1938."

In all 171 men had been working underground when the explosion occurred at 5.32am; the cause an ignition of coal dust spilling from one or more of the tubs of dust waiting to be taken to the pit bottom. The conclusion was that the explosion killed 79 and injured 40 was caused by some form of electric arcing, or sparks.

■This is Parkhouse Colliery mines rescue team in either the late 1940s or early 1950s. Unfortunately the only person I can name is my late father William H Roberts, who is second from the left on the back row. I recall as a child my father telling me that he had been in one of the teams involved in the Creswell Colliery disaster. I remember him taking me to the Mines Rescue Station in Chesterfield on one of their training days. I remember vividly one of the officers there demonstrating how cold the liquid oxygen used in the breathing apparatus was by immersing a piece of rubber tubing in the liquid and then dropping it on the floor where it shattered into pieces; fascinating. (Courtesy Roy Roberts)

Creswell Colliery

Tuesday 26 September 1950, is a day that will long be remembered in Creswell; the day when it became that village's turn to share in the true cost of coal. The banner headline in the Worksop Guardian declared: "CRESWELL'S SORROW SHARED. County wide expressions of sympathy – Mine Disaster Puts Our Area in Mourning".

The report read as follows: "It is our sorrowful duty this week to have to record the most serious mining disaster for many years. This occurred at Creswell Colliery on Tuesday when, following a fire underground 80 men were overcome by smoke and fumes. They were caught behind a barrier of flame, their escape impossible, and within a few hours came the official announcement that all hope had to be abandoned. Rescue efforts, carried on with total regard for personal safety so characteristic of the miner, were no further avail. It was realised before 12 noon that none of the men could be alive and further rescue attempts would inevitably lead to loss of life among the specially trained rescue teams who had rushed to the mine. From the time an underground worker reported the fire by phone to the surface, to the posting of a notice at the pit head stating that rescue workers were rapidly on the job, only eight hours had elapsed, but in spite of their efforts it was not possible to rescue any of the trapped men.

■ An anxious crowd of relatives, friends and neighbours awaits news in the pit yard. After the statement announcing that there was no hope for the men cut off by the fire, the Vicar of Creswell, the Rev C S Branson, led the crowd in prayer. (Sheffield Star)

■ The only way of extinguishing the fire and preventing it spreading though the workings was to seal it off and deny it air. Miners and volunteers filled sandbags to be used in the sealing off which would also mean abandoning the bodies of the dead until the flames were out. (Sheffield Star)

■ Rescuers bring NCB officials up to date with how the rescue attempt is going. Left to right are: Sir Hubert Houldsworth, Chairman of the East Midlands Division; Minister of Fuel and Power Philip Noel Baker; and Lord Hyndley, Chairman of the NCB. It was only possible for the rescuers to recover three bodies before the decision to seal the mine was taken. The seals were opened after twelve hours and another 44 bodies recovered. However the fire was not out and the area had to be resealed. It would be nearly a year before the remaining bodies could be recovered.

■ Creswell villagers pay their respects as one of the disaster's victims is buried. The majority of the 80 dead came from the village and some families lost more than one member. (Sheffield Star)

■ Creswell Disaster rescue team members at a presentation dinner held at the Station Hotel, Chesterfield. A direct result of the Creswell disaster – caused by the frictional overheating of a damaged rubber conveyor belt – was the replacement of all such belts throughout the mining industry with ones made from non-flammable PVC. The disaster was also a factor in the NCB banning workers under sixteen years of age from working underground. Analysis of the disaster and how the fire and smoke spread was a factor in the development of the 'self-rescuer' breathing mask; easily deployed in an emergency the mask converted carbon monoxide – the main killer in underground fires – into harmless carbon dioxide. (Courtesy D.Buxton.)

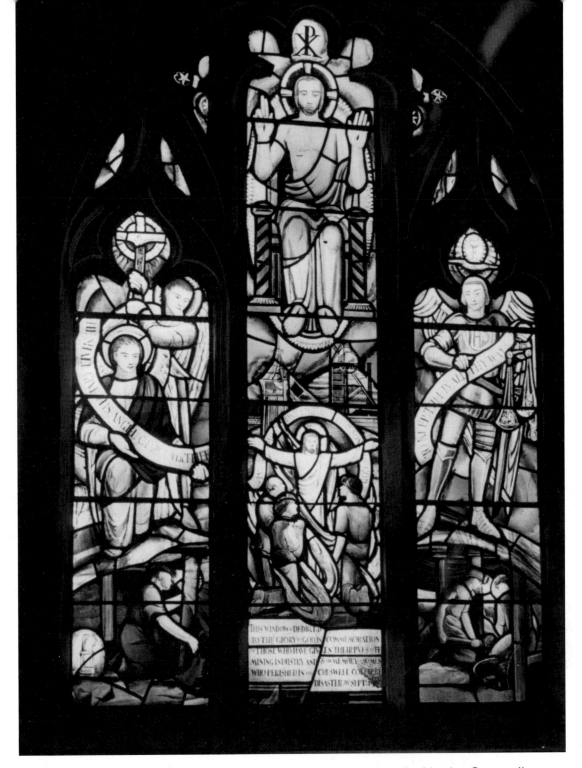

■ The parish church memorial window to the miners who died in the Creswell Colliery Disaster was officially unveiled during April 1952 by Sir Hubert Houldsworth and dedicated by the Assistant Bishop of Derby. The inscription reads: "Dedicated to the Glory of God and those who have given their lives to the mining industry, and in memory of 80 men who perished in the Creswell Colliery Disaster 26th September 1950."

■ Jack Turner, a survivor of the Creswell Pit Disaster. The picture was taken in September 1976. (Sheffield Star)

■ Glapwell Colliery Mines Rescue Team. (Courtesy Clive Pearce)

■ During the early 1960s the BBC made a documentary series titled Call to Action, one of which featured permanent staff from the Chesterfield Mines Rescue Service. The actual filming took place at the Grassmoor Training Centre. Here the director runs through the plot with members of the film crew and rescue squad.

Prior to the Second World War, Strand Films made a series of documentaries about British industries including mining. The underground film sequences were shot by Strand cameramen using clockwork cameras to reduce the risk of fire. (Courtesy D Buxton)

■ Despite the inevitable distractions of having a film crew watching their every move, the rescue team carried out their exercise to the book. (Courtesy D Buxton)

■ Emergency underground operating theatre in Markham No1 Colliery. (Courtesy D Buxton)

■ Members of the Markham Colliery Ambulance Brigade in camp at Skegness. (Courtesy D Buxton)

■ Members of the Mines Rescue Service at Infirmary Road Station, Chesterfield, c1965 onwards. Left to right: A Wright, G Colley (station officer), R Cartledge, T Halfpenny, P Mallen, F Skingle, E Mellish, G Swindell, T Griffiths, V Hind, G Wilkinson (station officer). (Courtesy Alan Wright)

Markham Colliery 1973

Markham's second twentieth century disaster occurred at No.3 shaft during winding operations on Monday 30 July 1973. At around 6.20am the double-decker cage was descending the 392 yards deep shaft carrying 29 men down to start their work.

Everything was going smoothly until the winding engine man applied the brakes. The routine was to make the brake application when the cage was about 100 yards from the pit bottom thereby allowing a steady final descent.
On this day however nothing happened. The brake had failed, the cage continued down at full speed and there was no way to stop it.

There was an additional problem. The haulage cable had cages at both ends so when one was going up, the other was going down. So as the descending cage was hurtling towards the pit bottom the cage on the other end was heading for the top of the shaft.

A safety devise was in place. The King system at the top of the shaft cuts the cable buts holds the ascending cage securely so it cannot fall back down the shaft. It worked. However, the inch thick heavy cable was under such tension that it whiplashed through the enginehouse causing a large amount of damage to the structure. Somehow the engineman, Dick Kennan, avoided the mayhem and following emergency instructions hit the emergency stop button thereby cutting the power. Though the power was cut there was no way of stopping the heavy cable and other debris falling down the shaft onto the stricken cage.

An inquiry later found that the accident had been caused by metal fatigue on the braking system.

■ The scene at No.3 shaft at around midday on 30 July 1973.

■ With No.3 shaft out of action a coal-winding shaft was pressed into service for man-riding and rescue work. Of the 29 men in the cage, 18 were dead and 11 seriously injured. Derbyshire Times reader Malcolm Cowley of Unstone, Dronfield, wrote: I am one of the survivors of the 1973 Markham pit disaster in which I suffered multiple injuries. The cage plunged to the bottom when all 14 devices failed. I was only 29 years old and have never been able to work since.

Another reader, Mr Clark, who at the time worked at Glapwell, recalled that his pit was chosen to trial a secure soft landing pad developed by the NCB. During trials the Glapwell cage was dropped at different speeds to access impact damage and survivability. The trials proved successful and soft landings were installed in all shafts in Derbyshire pits.

■ Arkwright Colliery Rescue Team on 26 May 1977 (Courtesy Alan Wright).

■ Arkwright ambulance team c1968. (Courtesy Alan Wright)

■ Not all accidents resulted in a turn out by mines rescue or the ambulance team.

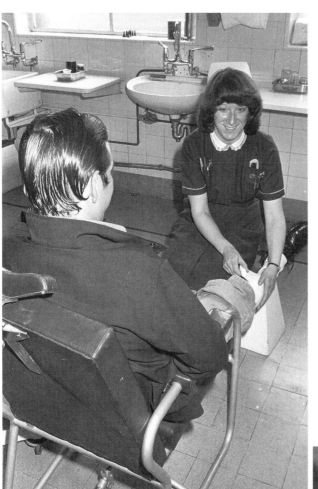

■ Close up from an ambulance competition c1987. The realistic looking injury was created using plasticine, cochineal and glass. The casualty was Alan Wright. (Courtesy Alan Wright)

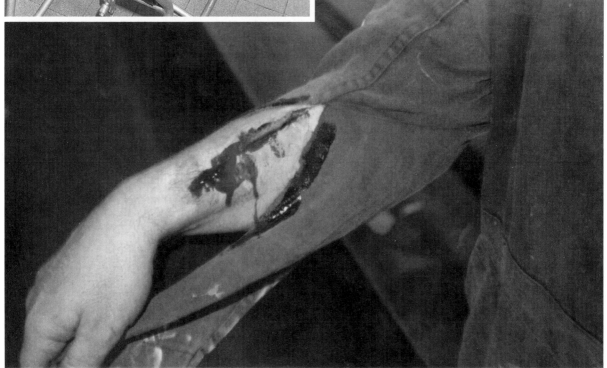

INDUSTRIAL UNREST

■ Major industrial action in the coal mining industry came in 1910-11 when 30,000 Welsh colliers struck over the complicated wage structure then in use. Colliers were paid according to price-lists negotiated at local level between their Federation lodges and the mine owners. A colliery price-list would offer a standard rate per ton of coal "got" from the face, with additional payments for work undertaken in "abnormal places". This could include working poor ground, variations in the seam and so on. There were also payments for repairing timbers and clearing dirt etc.

Following the Welsh miners strike, the fight for a minimum day wage for all colliers intensified with the Nottinghamshire and Yorkshire Federation lodges demanding a straight 8 shillings a day for coal hewers. The owners rejected the demand, though they did offer to guarantee the allowances for working in "abnormal places".

In a national ballot at the beginning of 1912, the colliers voted for a stoppage; the strike beginning at the end of February when the men at Alfreton Colliery came out. The strike was eventually settled with the passing of the Minimum Wage Act.

The next major strike involving mineworkers was the General Strike of 1926, and with a few minor exceptions industrial unrest on the coalfields remained dormant until January 1972 when the NUM under Joe Gormley came out in protest at a £2-a-week pay offer by the NCB.

■ Striking miners and their families, scour the spoil heaps of Brockwell Colliery, Chesterfield, for small pieces of coal during the strike of 1912 as their own supplies of coal had been cut off by their employers.

■ In 1926 Britain's mines were at a standstill due to industrial action over the colliery owners plans to extend the working week whilst at the same time reducing wages. On 4 May the TUC called a General Strike in support of the miners but they caved in to government pressure after only nine days when the home secretary declared the action might be unlawful. The miners fought on for another six months before giving up and returning to work. Our picture shows one of the many collection/distribution points where the families of striking miners could obtain bread.

■ History repeats itself as miners' families collect coal at Clay Cross during the 1972 strike. (Sheffield Star)

■ One of the few pits working in the entire country on 10 January 1972 was the privately operated Stratfield Colliery, Stretton, Clay Cross. (Sheffield Star)

■ Dennis Skinner MP lends his support at a rally by Derbyshire miners' wives. (Derbyshire Times)

■ One feature of the 1972 strike was the ability of the NUM to deploy 'flying pickets' to almost anywhere in the UK. By the middle of February, a number of power stations had shut due to lack of coal and those still operational were picketed. The Heath Government was on the rack, declaring a state of emergency and a three-day week. Our picture shows a group of flying pickets outside a coal depot. (Sheffield Star)

■ Derbyshire miners' victory rally held at Chesterfield. (Derbyshire Times)

■ The aftermath of the 1972 strike. A pit deputy inspects the damage in the Tipton D.10 supply gate at Bolsover Colliery. The stick he is holding is 3ft in length and was dual purpose; an aid to walking and a measuring instrument. (Sheffield Star)

■ World oil supplies were plunged into chaos during October 1973 when Egypt and Syria launched an attack on Israel on Yom Kippur, the Jewish Day of Atonement. The UK was still in crisis, inflation in double figures, and the TUC still in a combative mood over pay restrain. With perfect timing guaranteed once more to turn the screw on the Heath Government, the NUM submitted a pay demand more than double the government maximum, and then stuck the boot in by imposing an overtime ban. The miners had allies; both the power workers and railwaymen imposed their own overtime bans. 81 per cent of miners voted in favour of industrial action.

During December the government brought back the three-day-week and the following February Heath called his "Who governs Britain?" general election on union power. He was narrowly defeated by Labour.

Our picture, taken in early 1974, shows miners collecting coal for distribution to old age pensioners. (Sheffield Star)

■ The Thatcher Government came into office set both on revenge for the Edward Heath's humiliation at the hands of the miners and determined to crush trade union power and influence. The Tories were also committed to banning secondary picketing and the use of secret ballots for strike action.

MP Nicholas Ridley had been given the task of drawing up plans for confrontation. From the Governments point of view the ideal time for the miners to strike would be in early spring as the demand for coal and electricity would be starting to fall by then. Ridley recommended importing foreign coal and building up stocks especially at power stations. He also recommended that striking miners should be denied social security payments which would of course impact upon their families and put pressure on the men to return to work.

In 1982 NUM president, Joe Gormley was succeeded by Arthur Scargill and in 1983 Thatcher appointed the no nonsense Canadian mining man Ian McGregor to head the NCB. A clash of wills was almost inevitable.

In the twelve months prior to the 1984-85 strike, the NCB had closed 23 pits employing 21000 miners and it was estimated that if the NCB had its way as many as 100,000 jobs would be lost to the industry by 1988.

The catalyst for the strike came on 1 March 1984, when with total disregard for the agreed joint NUM/NCB colliery review procedure, the NCB announced that Cortonwood Colliery was to close in a matter of weeks. That the workforce at Cortonwood had previously been assured by the NCB that the pit was safe for at least five more years, or that money had been spent refurbishing parts of the colliery counted for nothing.

Within days most of the country's coal fields were idle; shut down by picketing miners from the most threatened pits. Derbyshire pits continued working as agreed until the outcome of their ballot on 14 March. The result by a narrow margin was against strike action however local NUM leaders ignored this and declared the strike official.

This picture was taken on Day 9 (Monday 19 March 1984) of the Miners' Strike and this is the scene outside the main gate at Bolsover Colliery. This was the last pit in Derbyshire to stop production.

■ Day 65 (Monday 14 May 1984) was the day of the Mansfield Rally when at least 10000 marched through the town and back to their starting point at the local leisure centre where they were addressed by Arthur Scargill (NUM President), Jack Taylor (NUM Yorkshire President), Peter Heathfield (NUM General Secretary), Bolsover MP and former miner Dennis Skinner and Chesterfield MP Tony Benn. (Sheffield Star)

■ On Day 129 (Tuesday 17 July 1984) between 800-1000 pickets had gathered at Shirebrook only to be confronted by around 1000 police including reinforcements from the MET. The use of these large mobile police squads had been recommended by Nicholas Ridley MP in his report to Thatcher on tackling the trade unions head on. Despite much pushing and shoving there were only two arrests.

■ Buses formerly used to carry working miners lie burnt out at Thompson Engineering, Pleasley Vale, Mansfield, August 1984. (Sheffield Star)

■ Dawn on Day 247 (Monday 12 November 1984) and a burnt out car is testament to a night which saw a fair amount of violence around Dinnington Colliery. (Sheffield Star)

■ Day 250 (Thursday 15 November 1984) of the Miners' Strike and the local welfare club at Shirebrook is almost deserted.

■ This was the scene at Shirebrook Colliery on Day 252 (17 November 1984) of the Miners' Strike. For some months working miners here had been ferried to and from work in 'armoured' buses. At the beginning of the strike the majority of the county's 14,500 NUM members had come out. Some joined the thousands of Yorkshire flying pickets outside Derbyshire pits; many more just stayed away.

Violence spilled over and strikers were blamed for physical assaults on miners who returned to work. As well as shouting threats, strike-breakers' houses and cars were damaged. Slowly however, more and more strike-breakers endured the journey into work, aboard mesh-protected buses, through lines of heckling pickets, flanked by massed police. By November 1984, 1157 men were working in north Derbyshire pits and by January 1985 more than half were back at work. At the time of the strike there were 11 NCB pits and two workshops in north Derbyshire. Today, they are all closed.

■ Christmas 1984 is approaching and with at least 100,000 miners still holding out this centre is busy making up food parcels for distribution to the families of striking miners in South Yorkshire/North Derbyshire. (Sheffield Star)

■ NUM president Arthur Scargill with Chesterfield MP Tony Benn. In the Sheffield Star in February 1989 Mr Benn said that government plans to import seven million tonnes of coal through new Humberside ports at Killingholme and Immingham would sign the death warrants of many mining communities and would have a catastrophic effect on the Chesterfield area, where 25 per cent of employment depended on the mining industry. Mr Benn called on trade unionists and councillors meeting in Chesterfield to mount a broad-based campaign to fight the Humberside Ports legislation then before Parliament. He also asked that local chambers of trade and commerce to get involved and for a conference to be called on the future of the local economy.

Opponents of the proposed new ports estimated that at least 20,000 jobs were at risk in coalfield communities stretching from Leeds to Leicestershire. Chesterfield Trades Union Council president Barry Johnson said Labour MPs had put up a stalwart fight in the committee stage of the Bill but a lot of trade unionists were still ignorant of the threats posed to jobs. He said if the privatisation of the electricity industry and the two ports went ahead North Derbyshire would be left with just one pit – Shirebrook. (Courtesy Clive Hardy)

■ This picture of Det Sgt Kieron Wright was taken by a Sheffield Telegraph photographer in early December 1984. He is holding a metal spike that allegedly pierced the cab roof of an NCB lorry carrying explosives to Renishaw Park Colliery.

■ Henry Richardson of the Nottinghamshire NUM arrives at the union's Sheffield headquarters for an executive meeting on 7 January 1985.

■ In January 1985 the Killamarsh women's action group undertook a thirty-mile trek around seven North Derbyshire pits. The following was published in the Derbyshire Times on 9 March 1990.

Derbyshire women were among the first to organise in support of the striking miners. A group set up by Chesterfield Labour Party to support Tony Benn's election decided to stick together and back the strike, and within days of the strike starting they had organised a soup run to miners on the picket lines. And, under the banner 'They shall not starve' they organised canteens and collection points for food and fuel.
Tom Vallins of Chesterfield Labour Party said the work done by the women was one of the most memorable aspects of the strike. "The women were marvellous," he said. "They were organising the food collections and speaking in support of the strike. It was amazing how they did it."

Those who did not know the mining communities were astonished by the women's valour but the women were the first to admit that they often surprised themselves.
Toni Bennett from Chesterfield Women's Action Group said: "It made women far more aware of their own capabilities."

Gordon Butler, secretary of Derbyshire NUM, described the sense of family tradition in the villages which the women were determined to preserve. "Women had always stood strong in the mining communities. You saw this in the pit disasters when they supported the widows and comforted the men," he said. "There had always been an inherent family atmosphere and when the women saw the threat of the break-up of their families they reacted instinctively."

Bolsover MP Dennis Skinner shared the platform with miners' wives and girlfriends at rallies up and down the country and is full of admiration for the way they spoke up for their communities.

He said: "I remember women on the platform who had never spoken before. One woman broke down in tears, she was very sorry for herself. They were going to make a collection after me but I said: "Have the collection now."

Many of the women have stayed in their action groups to support other disputes and causes such as the recent ambulance dispute.

Others are content to know that they stood beside their men for 12 months and fought for what they held most dear – the future of their children and their communities. (Derbyshire Times)

■ With no prospect of a negotiated settlement in sight, a NUM delegate conference held on 3 March voted by 98 votes to 91 to end the strike.

On 5 March the strike was over and thousands of men marched back to the Derbyshire pits after a year on strike, the longest national dispute in British industrial history. They returned with their heads held high but with heavy hearts and empty pockets. They had won nothing – except the respect of hundreds of thousands of people around the world. Here the men of High Moor Colliery return to work marching behind their NUM banner.

On 26 April High Moor was again at a standstill when miners walked out over working conditions claiming they were expected to work in up to four feet of water at the pit's most productive face. Austin Fairest, North Derbyshire area NUM president, said the NCB had refused to pay the face men extra for working in water. With the NCB refusing to negotiate until the men returned to work, Mr Fairest said: "We don't accept it is reasonable for the Coal Board to expect men to work in so much water. With today's technology it would be easy to pump the water away, but it is clear the union is being blamed for a deterioration in underground conditions because of the 12-month strike. It's the pit's most productive face and yet there is so much water in the heading the men can't work it to full capacity."

Though the NCB refused to discuss details of any offer with the Press, the NUM said that the men had been offered waders and £1 a day extra but had refused. The flooding problem was eventually sorted out but on 28 May, High Moor was once again at a standstill. This time it was due to pit deputies staging a 24-hour strike which was expected to affect all three shifts with about 500 NUM members being sent home. Local NACODS chiefs had called the High Moor men out after two colliery officials defied an overtime ban and worked over the Bank Holiday weekend. Area official Walter Burrows said: "I understand these men don't agree with the overtime ban. It doesn't matter whether they agree or not. They had the right to vote and the vote went against them." At the time there were 50 NACODS members at High Moor.

■ NUM President Arthur Scargill addresses union members at Whitwell Colliery. After Whitwell closed in 1986 the North Derbyshire Coalfield comprised Ireland, Arkwright, Renishaw Park, Warsop, Bolsover, Shirebrook, Markham, and High Moor collieries. After Measham closed in 1986, the South Derbyshire coalfield was down to just three pits; Cadley Hill, Rawdon, and Donisthorpe.

■ Bolsover NUM branch secretary Geoff Poulter lost his job as a branch official during the 1984-85 strike when working miners won control. A consequence of Bolsover miners automatically becoming members of the breakaway Union of Democratic Mineworkers was that Mr Poulter was told by the NCB that he faced the sack if he attempted to undertake any NUM business at the pit because only the UDM was recognised. Interestingly, though Bolsover was the only Nottinghamshire pit to vote against breaking with the NUM, Mr Poulter was forced to give up his office and set up in a bus shelter outside the pit gates. In November 1985 Mr Poulter told The Derbyshire Times that: "It's a bit cold at nights but its well worth it and I am certainly winning. What boosts us more than anything is that we now have 15 men signed up who worked throughout the strike. One or two people thought it was funny setting up an office outside the gates but I am deadly serious. If necessary we may have to use Tebbit's law to ensure we are allowed to join the union of our choice." Mr Poulter claimed that 361 out of 840 miners had signed up with the NUM. (Derbyshire Times)

■ Dozens of privately operated mines such as footrails (a typical example is depicted here; had continued production throughout the year-long miners' strike, as had some larger operations such as Doe Lea Colliery near Chesterfield.

END OF AN ERA?

■ On 5 February 2009, the Derbyshire Times ran a piece by Helen Beighton: "Return of King Coal". Coal mining is due to return to north Derbyshire after developers were given the green light to extract coal in preparation for major redevelopment work on an old industrial site.

Planning permission to extract around 130,000 tonnes of coal from the former Biwater Works site, off Market Street in Clay Cross, was granted by Derbyshire County Council last week.

Developer Maximus said that the coal mining is needed as part of an expensive clean-up operation of the contaminated site – which is now known as Silkston – to enable the building of new homes, offices, a hotel and public open spaces.

Bryn Hopkinson, commercial director for Maximus, said: "This decision is a major step forward in helping to realise our long-term regeneration vision for Silkston which will create significant new jobs and homes for Clay Cross.

"The current state of the economy has meant that activity has completely stopped on many development sites throughout the UK but we remain committed to this project. "We will be using income generated from the sale of the coal to fund the expensive clean-up of the site to ensure that our plans can continue on schedule."

Maximus is planning to form a liaison committee with local parish councils which will meet at regular intervals and make sure any issues that arise with the development can be addressed.

The company submitted a revised planning application to NE Derbyshire District Council late last year.

This proposal included plans for building around 950 homes, up to 29,500 square metres of employment space, a new hotel, a new link relief road to the north of Clay Cross high street and extensive public open space amenities.

■ Alfreton Colliery (1886-1968) was originally owned by the Blackwell Colliery Co who also owned Shirland, Blackwell "A" and Blackwell "B" collieries. The closure of Alfreton led to an adjournment debate in Parliament. At 4.4am on 9 April 1968, Raymond Fletcher, the MP for Ilkeston, spoke: "I find it a matter of regret that I have to welcome my hon. Friend the Minister of State, Board of Trade, to the Dispatch Box at this unearthly hour of the morning. Nevertheless I do welcome him, for we have never exchanged angry words since we were both elected, and I hope that he will not have any angry words to say in replying to this debate.

"In December, 1967, Alfreton Colliery closed and 560 men lost their jobs. Later Denby Hall Colliery closed and 500 men lost their jobs. I prefer to use the term "lost their jobs" instead of using the word "displaced" because I think it is more accurate. Now we have had the announcement that Swanwick Colliery will close in September, and this will cause another 770 men to lose their jobs.

"By September in this part of my constituency we shall have a problem of the size that I have mentioned. It fits into a larger problem and I think I can best outline the nature of the problem by referring to the evidence given by the Derbyshire County Council to the Hunt Committee. It is pointed out in this evidence that the Erewash Valley – that is a fancy way of describing my constituency – contained 22 collieries employing 17,000 miners in 1951, that by March 1967 there were six collieries employing 6,300 and that by 1970 there will be only two collieries employing 2,000. This is a massive rundown of a major industry and it has created tremendous problems for all people living in the area."

Blackwell workshops survived longer than the pits and when the decision to close them was announced in the press on 18 June 1985, it was slammed as an act of "callous indifference" by Bolsover MP Dennis Skinner. In a letter to area director Ted Horton, Mr. Skinner said the workshops had always been regarded as "a unique venture" because miners disabled in pit accidents were chosen for jobs there. Mr. Skinner said the closure was "outrageous" in an area of his constituency where the level of unemployment was extremely high.

"During the strike the Government and the NCB kept trotting out their assurances that anyone presently employed in the coal industry who wanted a job could have one," said Mr. Skinner.

"I would like to know where are the 240 vacancies in workshops or pitheads within reasonable travelling distance for the 240 now at Blackwell."

On 21 June the Sheffield Star announced that around half of the men had chosen voluntary redundancy and the remainder would be sent to workshops in Derbyshire and Nottinghamshire.

■ The closure of Teversal Colliery in 1980 might be one of the reasons why Nottinghamshire miners were reluctant to come out on strike in 1984. When the NCB announced Teversal's closure the Nottinghamshire NUM asked their National Executive in Sheffield for assistance in keeping the pit it open. They were turned down. When Nottinghamshire was asked to support action to save Yorkshire pits, it became a matter of: "You wouldn't help us so why should we help you?"

In 2007 test boring was carried out at Teversal with the view of accessing an outcrop of coal by means of a drift. carried out at Teversal with the view of accessing an outcrop of coal by means of a drift.

■ By February 1979 the eyesore that had once been Dinnington Main colliery tip had been landscaped.

■ The last men to come to the surface off the last shift at Brookhouse head for the baths. At the time the NCB was offering reasonably attractive redundancy payments. A man aged 49, in the industry since he was 16, would get about £1000 for each year of service, plus a lump sum, making a total of more than £36,000. For men over 50 conditions of voluntary redundancy or early retirement were a little more complicated, but with 30 years service a man aged 50 could expect a total lump sum of more than £22,000 plus about £79 a week. (Sheffield Star)

■ Frank Spowage, Brookhouse Colliery, 25 October 1985. (Sheffield Star)

■ It wasn't long before the demolition men moved in at Brookhouse; here the colliery chimney bites the dust. (Sheffield Star)

■ In the wake of the 1984-85 strike colliery closures and demolition became an all too familiar sight.

On 26 November 1985, the Morning Telegraph reported that on the previous day the NUM had released a list of 121 collieries whose future the union claimed must be in doubt. The list was based on pronouncements in the National Coal Board's New Strategy for Coal that competitive coal must cost no more than a certain amount to produce. The union's journal, The Miner, stated that 42 of the threatened pits were in Yorkshire, 15 in Nottinghamshire and seven in Derbyshire.

The alarm sprang from a paragraph in the NCB strategy document whish stated: "It is most unlikely that any colliery constantly producing an operating cost in excess of £1.65 per gigajoule could make an economic contribution even if supply and demand is in balance." An important factor at the time was that the NUM list was based on NCB operating results for the six months to 29 September 1985, the period immediately following the year-long strike when many pits had been left standing with no maintenance cover.

The NCB told the Morning Telegraph that the production costs quoted in The Miner could "not possibly support the union's claim of butchery throughout the industry."

During the last week of February 1986 the NCB announce a £33million investment programme for North Derbyshire pits including: £6.5million for Markham for underground improvements and seam development; £4.3million for High Moor for investment in surface and underground drift operations; £3.8million for Shirebrook for the development of seams, plus surface improvements; £2.8nmillion for Bolsover for seam development; £300,000 for Warsop for a computer control system. NCB Area Director, Ted Horton also said that £7million of the investment was earmarked for new equipment. Mr Horton also told union officials that the Coal Board's policy of no redundancies would result in a new recruitment campaign at some pits.

In exchange for the investment North Derbyshire's surviving nine collieries were expected to sell 7.3million tonnes of coal and make a profit of £15million in the 12 months after April 1986, but to achieve this target production costs would have to be kept to a minimum in order to compete successfully with other energy sources.

Mr Horton told the unions that: "Eighty-seven per cent of our production will continue to be supplied to the electricity generating market, but we shall also endeavour to maximise sales in other higher priced outlets. With this aim in mind, 1986/87 will be a year of uncompromising attitudes towards high quality standards." Mr Horton said that he expected the Area to continue employing just over 9300 men for the coming year and told employees that: "Provided there are no major changes in the market situation, or in expected costs of production, the assurance of no compulsory redundancies, together with an opportunity for recruitment at some locations will continue."

NUM treasurer John Burrows welcomed the news of the Coal Board's intention to invest locally. "We are pleased in the suggested activities in the Area for the next twelve months and we hope the projections are successful because it means retaining the life of the pits in North Derbyshire and the jobs of our members."

Investment or not by the end of 1995 all the county's deep mines would silent.

■ Dennis Skinner MP with campaigner Brenda Nixon at the women against pit closures rally held at Doncaster on 27 February 1993. (Sheffield Star)

■ Dennis Skinner MP and Rodney Bickerstaffe of the National Union of Public Employees (NUPE) join the protest march against pit closures. (Sheffield Star)

■ This picture of children each holding a placard bearing the name of a colliery closed following the end of the year-long miners' strike was taken during the 1993 rally against pit closures. Among the names are a number of Derbyshire and Nottinghamshire pits including: Arkwright, Creswell, Renishaw Park, Warsop, Gedling, Linby, Babbington, and Mansfield.   (Sheffield Star)

■ Just three days to the miners march for jobs in London and the announcement came that Shirebrook was to close, something the workforce had been suspecting since the previous October. Michael Heseltine's announcement that the pit would be mothballed and/or offered to private operators was treated by many with the contempt it probably deserved. To make matters worse, when Heseltine's announcement was broadcast on TV, John Major could be seen sitting twiddling his thumbs.

■ Miners march through London on 29 March 1993. (Sheffield Star)

■ Among those marching in support of the miners included: the actress Paola Dionisotti, Only Fools and Horses actor Roger Lloyd Pack, and Norman Willis. (Sheffield Star)

■ No.2 winding tower is demolished at Warsop.

■ One of the deepest mines in the country, Bevercotes Colliery was only sunk during the late 1950s yet it too no longer exists. Richard Alexander the Tory MP for Newark was a Thatcherite but nevertheless he fought against the pit closures and gained a reputation as a serial rebel voting against his own government on no less than six occasions. When challenged over his actions, he explained that he could not, in all consciousness, bring himself to vote for policies that would throw thousands of people out of work.

■ Bearing a wreath, members of the Bolsover branch of the NUM march behind their union banner depicting Arthur Scargill's arrest at Orgreave during the 1984-85 strike, to the colliery entrance where the wreath was placed. In 2004, Chesterfield councillor Bill Flanagan, chairman of the national Coalfields Communities Campaign, said: "If miners had won the strike I think there would have been a more sensible run-down of closures."

He said coal that would have lasted 100 years has been buried in the closed pits, and Britain could find itself in a "hostage" position in the future, having to import fuel from overseas.

■ Abandoned houses became an all too familiar scene in the former pit villages of Notts and Derbyshire as men moved away in search of work.

PATRONS (cont'd)

NAME		COLLIERY	FROM	TO
M	Fletcher	Markham	1962	1993
Patrick	Garvey	Markham	1966	1993
M A	Gascoyne	Markham	1963	1993
Cliff	Gibbs	Donisthorpe	1977	1990
T	Gray	Bolsover	1955	1989
Mick	Greenall	Arkwright	1957	1988
Michael	Gregory			
Derek Walter	Gurney	Highmoor	1980	1997
Maria	Guzvic			
Stephen	Hall	Bolsover	1974	1993
Mark	Hancock	Markham 2	1983	1993
Christopher	Hardy	Renishaw Park	1981	1988
Michael Stuart	Hardy	Markham 1, 4, Black Shale	1980	1993
R J	Harper	Shirland	1957	1962
David	Hart	Grassmoor, Markham	1957	1993
Michael	Hart	Bolsover	1974	1993
R	Hawkins	Markham	1969	1989
H J	Haywood	Markham	1943	1975
Samuel	Henson	Markham 1	1954	1989
Raymond	Henstock,	Holmewood, Arkwright	1959	1975
T	Hill	Grassmoor, Shirebrook	1960	1992
Mrs J	Hind			
Mrs M	Hodgson			
Graham	Hooper	Markham		
Robin	Howdle	Arkwright	1967	1988
Keith	Hunt	Morton	1947	1963
Andrew	Jacques	Silverhill		
George Maurice	Jacques	Silverhill		
Ralph	Johnson	Markham 1-4	1957	1992
Bernard A	Jones	Glapwell, Markham	1954	1985
Eric	Jones	Williamthorpe Mobile Plant Pool	1978	1988
Andrew	Jones			
Kevin	Kew	Ireland, Markham	1977	1992
John Barry	Keyworth	Markham 4	1972	1993
David	King	Ireland	1958	1993
James	Kirkwood	Glapwell	1972	Closure
Bill	Kitchener	Ireland		
David	Larkin			
Everet	Lowe	Markham	1980	1993
Brian	Martin	Various collieries	1957	1990
Lynn	McBride	Markham		
Jim	McMahon	Markham 2		
Colin	Medlam	Whitwell		
Mr	Mellish	Mines Rescue Station	1968	1986
Ian Richard	Metcalfe			
Paul	Miles	Markham		
Brian	Mundy	Grassmoor, Morton, Holmwood, Markham	1951	1964
Stephen	Myronko	Highmoor, Kiverton, Thoresby	1985	1994
Cyril Colin	Neale	Markham 2	1952	1985
Barry	Nuttall			
Paul	Orton	Markham	1979	1987
Joseph	Owen	Markham 2	1935	1980
Barry	Peach	Arkwright	1957	1986
David	Pearson	Arkwright, Markham	1977	1991
Tony	Pick	Markham 2	1962	1993
Roy	Pickering	Williamthorpe	1953	1964
J F	Pollard	Holmewood, Bolsover	1942	1985